Contents

Your senses

You have five senses. They are seeing, hearing, touch, taste and smell. When you eat a lolly, messages about the colour, shape, taste and smell of the lolly are sent to your brain.

Ummm... this lolly tastes and smells delicious.

My Healthy Body

Senses

T.

Books

First published in the UK in 2002 by
Chrysalis Children's Books
An imprint of Chrysalis Books Group Plc
The Chrysalis Building, Bramley Road
London W10 6SP

Paperback edition first published in 2005

ISBN 1 84138 407 0 (hb)
ISBN 1 84458 273 6 (pb)

British Library Cataloguing in Publication Data
for this book is available from the British Library.

Design: Bean Bog Frag Design
Picture researcher: Terry Forshaw
Consultant: Carol Ballard

Printed in China

10 9 8 7 6 5 4 3 2 1

(T) = Top, (B) = Bottom, (L) = Left, (R) = Right.
Picture acknowledgements:All Photography by Claire Paxton
 with the exception of:5 © Bubbles/Geoff Du Feu; 8 ©
Bubbles/Frans Rombout; 9 © Chrysalis Images; 11 (T) © Bubbles/
Jacqui Farrow; 12 © Bubbles/Anthony Dawton; 13 © Bubbles/
Frans Rombout; 19 © Bubbles/Jennie Woodcock; 22 ©
Bubbles/Frans Rombout; 23 © Powerstock/Zefa; 25 (T)
© Bubbles/Frans Rombout; 26 © Bubbles/Loisjoy Thurston;
28 © Bubbles/Margaret Kalms.

Snowflakes feel
cold and wet.

Your brain takes in information
about all the things you do.

Your brain

Every day your brain takes in messages about the things you see, hear, smell, touch and taste. It sorts through all this information to tell you what is going on all around you.

Your brain has two halves. The right side is better at drawing. The left side is better at sums.

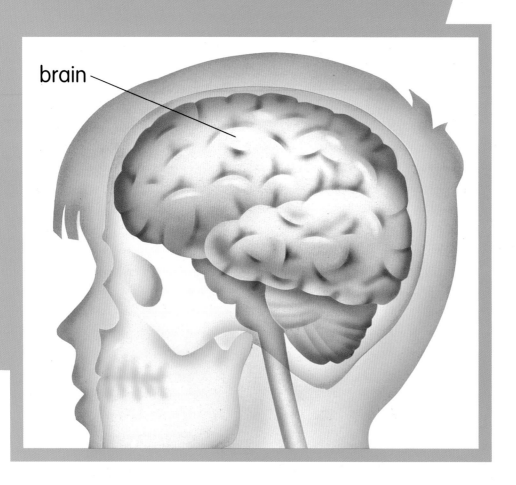

brain

Your brain is inside your head.

Your brain controls everything you do, from talking and laughing to playing games.

When you paint a picture, your eyes send messages to your brain about the colours you are using.

How do you see?

When you look at something,
light shines into your eye.
Your eye sends messages to
your brain and your brain works
out what you are looking at.

What can you
see when you
look through
the window?

The dark part of your eye is called the pupil. The coloured part is called the iris.

Your eyes allow you to see all the beautiful things around you.

How do you hear?

Sound travels through the air until it reaches your ears. Then it travels down a tube and into your head. Inside your head, a message is sent to your brain to tell you what the sounds are.

Your brain can tell you where a sound is coming from.

Your ears take in all the different sounds you hear.

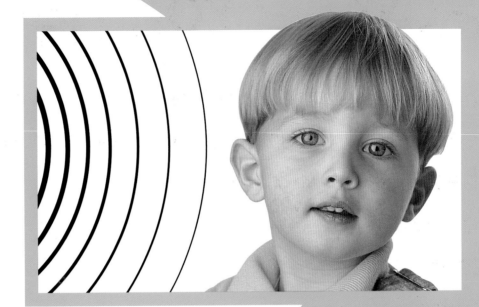

A whisper is a very quiet sound.

Never poke anything into your ears – they are very delicate.

Taking care

Your eyes, ears and brain are very precious. Wear sunglasses to protect your eyes in bright sunshine and never look straight at the sun.

When you are out rollerskating or cycling, wear a helmet to protect your head.

Loud sounds can damage your ears. Wear earmuffs to protect them.

Very cold weather can hurt your ears. A hat will keep them warm.

This boy is having his eyes tested to see if he needs glasses.

All about taste

Your tongue sends messages to your brain to tell you what food tastes like. Your tongue can sense four tastes: sweet, sour, salt and bitter.

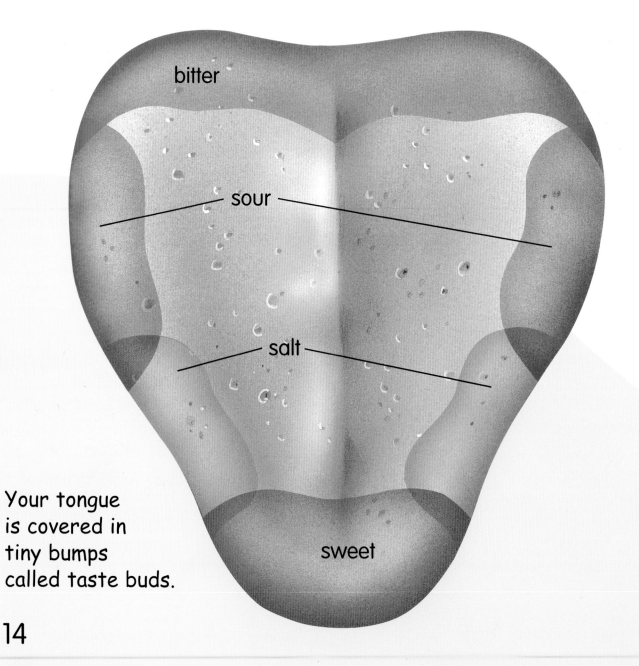

bitter

sour

salt

sweet

Your tongue is covered in tiny bumps called taste buds.

14

Chocolate biscuits taste sweet. Your sweet taste area is at the front of your tongue.

The back of your tongue can sense bitter flavours, like lemon peel.

When you eat, your tongue moves around in your mouth and helps you to chew your food properly.

What's that smell?

When you smell, air moves around inside your nose. Your nose sends messages to your brain, and your brain works out what you are smelling.

Your senses of taste and smell work together. Hold your nose while you eat. Does the food taste the same as usual?

Freshly-baked bread smells delicious.

Unwashed socks smell horrible!

Your sense of smell warns you about things that might be harmful, such as fire and smoke.

All about touch

When you touch something your skin tells you what it feels like. Ice is cold and water is wet. Bricks are hard and glue is sticky. Your skin gives you your sense of touch.

What do apples feel like? Are they hard or soft, rough or smooth?

A cat's fur feels
smooth and soft.

Your skin is very useful.
It bends when you do
and it's waterproof!

Feeling pain

If you touch something hot and burn your finger, you move your finger quickly. That's because a message is sent to your brain telling you that your finger hurts. Ouch that's hot!

Pain is your body's way of telling you that something bad is happening.

This girl has just pricked her finger on a cactus. She moves her hand away quickly.

Your mouth and lips are very sensitive. They will tell you if a drink is too hot.

Your reflexes

A reflex is an action you do without thinking. Swallowing and blinking are reflex actions. Babies are born with some reflexes that disappear as they grow older.

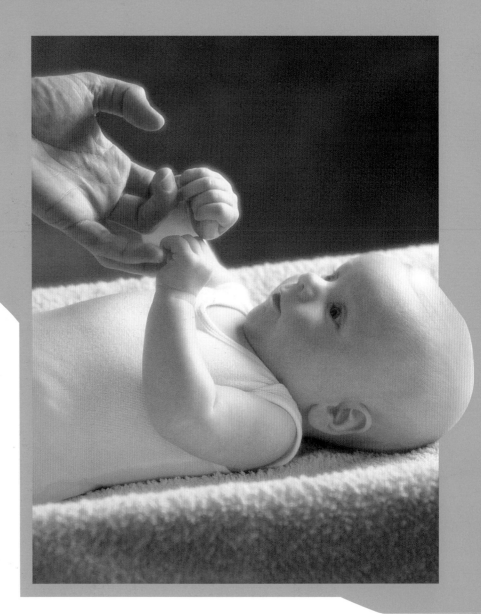

A baby will grab your finger and hold it tightly. This is a reflex action.

This doctor is testing a baby's reflexes. When she taps the baby's leg below the knee, the bottom half of the baby's leg jumps up.

Coughing is also a reflex action.

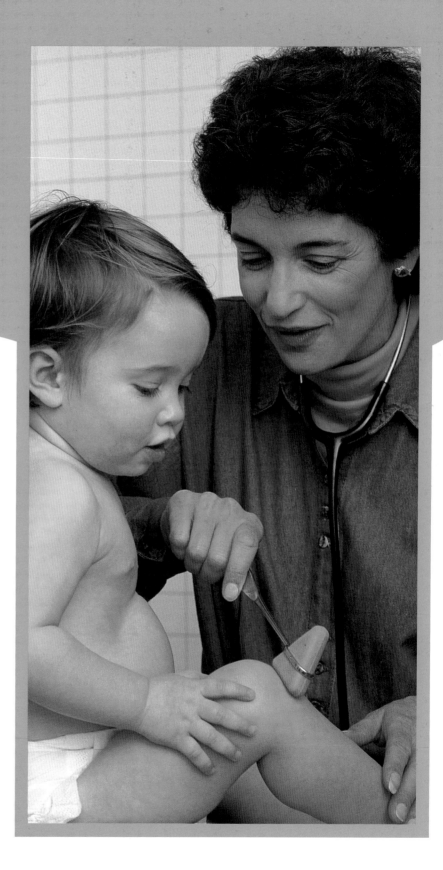

Balancing act

When you are playing a ball game, messages are sent to and from your muscles to your brain. The messages make sure that you throw and catch the ball without losing your balance.

Keep your eyes on the ball!

This baby is learning to walk. Every now and then she loses her balance and topples over.

Try standing on one leg. Can you balance?

Different parts of your body work together to help you to balance.

Learning new skills

We learn new skills by doing things over and over again. The more you practise something, the easier it becomes.

If you practise riding a bike, you will soon be able to do it without thinking.

Your memory can help you to remember new skills, such as riding a bike.

Can you remember how to tie your shoelaces?

To learn how to write, you must practise making the shapes of the letters.

27

Sleep

Sleep is very important. It gives your body time to rest and recover from all the exciting things you have done during the day.

Babies sleep for about 20 hours a day.
An adult sleeps for about 7-8 hours.

Can you remember your dreams? Some dreams are scary, but happy dreams about parties and Christmas are fun to remember.

When you begin to yawn, you know it's time for bed!

Words to remember

earmuffs
Pads that are worn over the ears to keep them warm and to protect them from loud noises.

delicate
Something that can be easily damaged or hurt.

muscles
Bundles of soft, stretchy fibres inside your body that make you move.

practise
To do something over and over again.

precious
Very special.

protect
To look after.

sensitive

To know how to tell the difference between things that are wet and dry, hard and soft and so on.

taste buds

Parts of your tongue that pick up flavours.

reflex

An action that you do without thinking.

skill

Something that you can do well, such as riding a bike or rollerskating.

waterproof

Something that doesn't let in water.

Index